A Scarred Republic

By Kerrod McNeal

In Loving Memory of Mary Artis

Welcome to A Scarred Republic

Read me

The day has now drawn to end

The decision has been made

Questions answered

The trivial now a reality

I pick words out of the air as a child picks their nose

Not knowing if I myself am at fault

My reputation precedes me

I'm not sure if that's necessarily a good thing

Because they may restrict me from my environment and everything else that encompasses my very being

With that being said I question my own feelings

Taking them off pause

Moving toward repeat because this feeling that I find myself feeling is hard to shake and has ruined not only my day but the rest of my year

I refuse to cry tears because as a child I was not geared this way

I was taught to be tough and laugh emotion and feelings in the face

This has since replaced my heart

Because I'm too preoccupied with what everyone else cares about and not myself

I'm too far-gone because I know that help is needed

Yet I do nothing to attain it.

I don't know exactly how it happened but I'm pretty sure how it will end

Not by the lines on the paper

Or the ink running out of this pen

I share these thoughts with the world because it is somewhat therapeutic to self and allows me to free my mind

If only for a moment from the burdens I carry

I'm not trying to escape them

But ultimately embrace what I am and what I have become

I would tell you the story verbally

But it's better to be read, than experience off the tip of my tongue

0 (Zero)

Ridicule fueled thoughts

Anxiety driven conjecture

My voice flutters across the crowd

Piercing their very being

Devouring the souls of my enemies

The winding spirits acknowledge the delivery of my word

To the ears of the non-believers

Tears fill my eyes

For a reason that is not apparent to the audience

But obvious to me

I have pushed myself toward the trees

It all seems as if it will pay off

I dare not count my eggs before they hatch

I'd rather play with the chicks

Once filled with so much anger it began to create a void inside me

I've since then moved to a different point in my own progression and I've found happiness in a way...

I rather not name it

Because I fear it will go away

Leaving me confronted by misery

And forced to relive those harsh days, that I've long forgotten...

A mere piece in the puzzle of life

To understand each of our own stories

In contrast to the bigger picture

We sometimes ignore it

Because it is this, which brings us, shame

It is irreprehensible

What the world has become

The rich will always be

But the poor are evolving

Opening up the flood gates of knowledge and prosperity

Searching for what is believed to be

A better life

I question this and it's postulates

I've removed the edges clean off the paper

Which limits the cuts

Since my life is like an open sore, that seldom heals

I go on and questions things that I don't agree with

Because in the end I trust what I feel

Closed Eyes

Closed eyes

No intentions of opening them

Just laying enjoying the quiet

I imagine a time when we never were and I reached out for you and felt nothing

This is because that's what I was before you came into my life

I was nothing more then a hollow case that has been filled with your love

Love means different things to different people

But when I think of love

All I see is you...

I look away in disbelief and back again

And yet you remain

Not only have you conquered my heart

But my brain has also become a causality of your endless beauty

That extends a smile from ear to ear

I can't help but imagine more for us

And I welcome it because I feel that it should be this way

I'm not sure if my prayers have been totally answered

But I know he got the idea of the message

When he set you in my life.

Basically what I'm trying to say is I love you and I never want to stop

If I could express love in drops

Then I would be your ocean

You would be my sun

Because you light up my life and thru the clouds your rays
would shine out feeding the world...

Blah

I laid my head on the clouds and threw my pillow in the sky

I just wanted to be accepted

But instead I was ostracized

I took a bath in the sea and sailed in my tub

What life is worth living if you never experience love?

I drank from the Milky Way and watched cows cross the sky

I can't do this by myself

I'm sure I won't survive

I unplugged the Sun and screwed bulbs in the sky

I wish I were free like a bird

I'd be so happy if I could fly...

I had a cold date

Luckily I ate a hot lunch

People never have fun anymore with life the world is out of touch...

Abstract Thoughts

Divorced but never married

Salaried yet never paid

These shades shield me from the suns harsh rays

These days end quickly

The pity of ones own guilt fills the space once thought to hold
a heart

This has left me beside myself

Which in itself is a feat

I walk away not looking back or responding to those calling my
name

They see me differently

Yet I feel the same

We all point fingers

But who's really the blame?

The more we change the more we stay the same

I aim for the clouds but barely seem to leave the ground.

I rather not blame gravity

It is excuses that hinder progression

Life lessons skipped

And what is meant is seldom said

Words get twisted like dreads

We lie then cry when caught and beg for forgiveness

Not from the person we wronged

But from ourselves

These fundamental ideas are more complicated than we all thought

Notations have been made

Friends lost

Enemies embraced

I taste nothing

Because it is my mouth that is dry

Leaving the mind thirsty for more

We hide behind closed doors

And the apple is rotten to the core

A Sphere

Sarcasm fills the room with voices other than my own

Which stir my thoughts away from self

I once thought that love was nothing more than a cruel trick

Blind

Suffering causing me to feel these feelings that makes me feel helpless without her beside me

Whether it is her touch, her smell, and her soothing embrace

I use to lay her head on my chest her hair semi-tangled as my fingers attempt to maneuver through each strand

I sometimes reminisce about thoughts of her bosom snugly upon my chest, causing many sleepless nights

Contradictions made allegations forgotten

All I see is we at the beginning middle and end of the day

It's not the same

My conscious whispers in the left ear the right ear corrupted not sure what the response will be

I compare my life to the clouds because when you look off into the sky the picture is not exact

Making it subject to interpretation

Kind of how I view some of the things I've gone thru...

I'm sure it can be argued that they were necessary in the evolution of my being

With that being said why is the usual motivation for greatness associated with suffering

JK Rowling's, Tyler Perry, Oprah Winfrey and soon myself

I dare not list my name

I'd rather blend in with the crowd

Generalizing my own heartache

Causing the audience to truly feel my pain

My message has now been delivered

Just know that by reading some of my thoughts that we have helped each other in some way...

I'm not saying you'll be a different person

I'm saying that your mind has been freed

Allowed to revolve in a complete revolution of a sphere

And you have subconsciously witnessed my struggle

We are all pieces to his puzzle and one day it will be completed and that is why we pray for better days

Because hope is needed

Blank

Cranium exposed

Its case empty

Pale...

Thoughts leaking on to the surface of life

Mislead thoughtless misguided neurotic

Ethnocentric

Urban myth

Full of disdain

Exoskeleton compromised

Sweaty palms

Tank on empty

Mind overload apparent

Transparent ideals

In the minds vacuum completely sucked in

Totally unearthed

Because I wasn't rooted in my position

Which has abruptly changed

Here I lay unprepared and overexposed to the world

Ultraviolet rays combing my body

The embrace warm

I'm not sure if I should trust it

Still torn

From night till morn

It pops

But it's not corn

It cries

Yet it's not born

Eye of a hurricane

When we're way past the storm

I reach out and feel an awkward gesture reach back at me

Paralyzed by fear

Compelled by curiosity

All this time on display for their enjoyment

That's why they wouldn't respond to me

(I'm dead)

I don't exist

My thoughts continued long after the bullet hit

I'm blank

Despondent

Hands drenched in disdain my heart sinks the phone rings

Even though I don't answer I know it's not for me. How can it be, if I never gave out the number?

Blood pressure one hundred eighty over nothing

I seldom make the right choices

These voices won't leave me be

Instead they whisper their opinions in my ear, utterly making me opinionated, which I'd rather not be

But it's the only way that I can maintain a balance

The odometer is broken by choice

I'd rather it remain this way because I don't want to know how many miles have been accumulated over time

I view it as contempt of self and the selfishness of my ways supersede my curiosity of the matter

I've endured terrible things like love, friendship and worst of all happiness they're just facades that will never be

How can a person that doesn't even love themselves, seek love from others company give love back?

They cannot

Which leads to nothing

Which is what we as a people have become

Over time

Because we worry about things that we can't change

Instead of the now

Which typical gets addressed later

Which leaves me

Despondent

Breakdown

Optimum precision exact movement

Timing off

Moment lost

Never to be recaptured...

A fluke a mistake a glitch in the scheme of things

Time stands still

Reminiscing about things that never happened

A delayed response

Muttering words

No recollection

Ambiguous terms

Misguided ideals

Heart felt talks

Algebraic equations that lead to nothing

You had me at hello

Then why did you say goodbye?

An empty nest made of falsehoods

Weaved with lies

The terms of his conception not easily mentioned

My heart weighs heavy...

Life full of disdain

Pain subtracts my true interaction with the ideals of the current situation

No reset button

Trapped in a open area

Drowning in nothingness

Found without you

Lost with you...

My own freedom sacrificed

The longer I remain

Why can't I walk out that door?

It's been determined

That the mind was assaulted

Basically fucked

But the body left pure

Breakdown (Extended)

Optimum precision

Exact movement

Timing off

Moment lost

Never to be recaptured

A fluke

A mistake

A glitch in the scheme of things

Time stands still

Reminiscing about things that never happened

A delayed response

Muttering words

No recollection

Ambiguous terms

Misguided ideals

Heart felt talks

Algebraic equations that lead to nothing

You had me at hello

Then why did you say goodbye?

An empty nest

Made of falsehoods

Weaved with lies

The terms of his conception not easily mentioned

My heart weighs heavy

Life full of disdain

Pain subtracts my true interaction with the ideals of the current situation

No reset button

Trapped in a open area

Drowning in nothingness

Found without you

Lost with you...

My own freedom sacrificed the longer I remain

Why can't I walk out that door?

It's been determined

That the mind was assaulted

Basically fucked

But the body left pure

I've endured many things

All better than this

I give at the right times

You never give at all

I feel confined to my own mind

Because you never try

I wonder why love is what you speak of

Yet all you do is cause me pain

Your feelings are just that

Your feelings

Because

If you felt what I feel then it would be mutual

Instead of this

Your selfishness has divided us more than you can imagine

And I can't imagine how we ever got here

I remember a day when you cared so much

That my body would quiver at the thought of your touch

Unequal Balance

An unequal balance a forced challenge

Car over the hill high mileage

Why be violent when you can give greetings

We all speak big words with no meaning

We're all feeding but off what?

No reason for your reaction

Except you feel it in your gut

Subject to the misery of the mind and the shortcomings of the body

Oddly enough we continue

On a fixed venue amazed by the physical but misled by the mental

Visual impairments

Cause the causality of the situation

To lead us to recreation

And penetration of ones imagination

These sensations are not by our own fault

But are taught at young ages

We are children that don't ever grow up

We just learn to our lives in different stages

What is change?

In less than a month

My life will change forever

I haven't the slightest idea what I'm doing

That makes it even better

He's soft small and loves my voice

His smile is pure

Priceless

His happiness is not forced

I look into his eyes and know there is still hope for me

I did something beautiful

This day I never thought I would see

A combination of two radically different halves

I'm not good at arithmetic

But I attempt to do the math

23 +23 = 46

Divide that by many

It equals the same shit

But when you multiple that a whole bunch of times the combination smiles at you and other times it cries

I've been unearthed

Excavated from my place

It's as if the world stands still

When I look into his face

God has winked in my direction and I'm not sure what to do. I can hear the voices whispering trying to give me clues

I'm back they said

Here is your chance don't be afraid

They will scatter like ants

I reached out

Eyes shifted

Voice full of pain

I dropped to my knees holding him up

Asking God to tell me his name

Then I heard a soft echo

If that even makes sense

He told me to look in the mirror

I did

I only saw myself

He makes complicated things easy

The trick is you have to know

When to ask for help

True Love

Love is something that you just can't forget about

That word that's on the tip of your tongue and you can't seem to spit it out

Feelings of compassion and comfort that two souls share

When you're in the presence of your other half

And there is nothing in the world you care about...

Love is those extra minutes in the day

That seem to last forever

Love is the best and worst feeling that one can experience...

No matter how much preparation

We're never truly prepared

Because love is like a thief in the night

Once it takes your heart

It's gone

When love goes away you can tell

Because you connect with the slowest saddest songs...

If love were a balloon

I'd release it into the air

For it to go to the top of the clouds and then it would be for the whole world to share

If I could describe love in one word

Then her name would you

Because as these words flow on to this screen

It's because I'm thinking of you

A Scattered Vision

I used two calculators

But things still didn't add up

I thought I asked the right questions

But the answers made zero sense

I put my hands in warm clay

But it will never be cement

I'm surrounded by many people

But I have only one friend

I read the book back to front

Because I never wanted it to end

The musician said lend me your ear

But then I'd only have one left

I don't want to be handicapped

Life would be so empty

If I were deaf

I'll tell you what I believe

If you can answer my questions

Is there really a God?

If so

Is he really omnipresent?

So is he watching me write this?

Then he knows how it's going to end

The sky is still blue

Water wet

In a mans' last hours

He spends them reflecting and full of regret

Pick up the pieces

Take a picture

Imagine life with no end

Then you will be able to picture the beginning and it will start all over again

This is my truth

Damn

Damn

I can't breathe

It's as though I'm constricted

Forced into this tight space

My face is not visible because there is no light

My thoughts come and go

Their relevance is no longer relevant to my situation

Can anyone explain?

Why the irony of life

Has now become the irony of my situation?

I know I haven't always been faithful

But I loved her

You would think that was enough

But now I find myself being treated like the others

And I cannot allow this

My bags are packed

I finally think it's time for me to go

I'm not sure of where I will go

Or if I will ever come back

I just know that here is not meant for me

Because if it was

I wouldn't have to question it

It would feel like home

But it doesn't

After so many years

You would think that my key fit the lock

But I find myself ringing the bell

And it's not because there isn't anyone home

Because

They're wide-awake

And this is what troubles me

It's as though they don't know my face or remember my name

I guess

It's better this way

Because God has a plan for me

And I don't pretend to know what it is

I just know it's not this...

Deserted

Dried mouth

Eyes flooded with tears

The ambiance of the whole mood disturbed

The wind still

A chill present at the arch of my back

I beg the voice from within to remain there

My happiness comes at a cost

I fear the worst is yet to come

I pray to God that I am further up on the list of those who he favors

Because I need his help quickly

An advisor won't due at this point

I make it my point to acknowledge my surroundings

For they have become different than what I'm use to

It's actually nice here

No longer subject to the harsh screams

Hustling back and fourth

Only to lose what you cared for in the first place

Memoirs of misery are what I now publish

Because even pain needs an audience

Mindset

Mindset like Potpourri

Glade plug in thoughts

Scented candles

Dropped ceilings

Lost salvation

Mind overload

Embalmed with nonsense

Transcended to oblivion

Misunderstood from the very beginning

Questioned to the end

Cry me something other than a river

Why not an ocean?

Limited success

Diluted dreams

Low fat ambition

I cringe at what we have become

Disillusioned in our own minds

Full of these idiosyncrasies

That keeps us apart

Transparent ideals that encompass nothing more than what
we can see beyond our fingertips

Bathtub memories

In a world full of showers

Tend to get washed away

I was told that the storm is over and that peace and prosperity
will come.

Then how come

We claim to live in states that are united

When the people that dwell them remain divided

We police the world and speak of a free land but our shortcomings we hide it

Divided we fall

Because only the poor and the minorities seem to march on

To secure freedoms and liberties that we ourselves don't truly have

Math is more than just 1+2

It is the sum of things that make us whole

The completeness of an individual

To be bigger than the moment

To let the petty situations of life go...

Only then will we be free,

Weighed down with the sins of life

I don't think you see

That's why when we pray

We're usually on our knees

Change

The History that was made today was not limited to only Black and White Americans

But is to be shared by all Americans

We have finally taken the necessary steps

To live up to the name that has represented this country in the world abroad

We are now that much closer to truly being The United States of America

This day will never be forgotten

Remember where you were when history came rushing in

Crashing down the walls

That has divided us for so long

The word "can't" has officially been replaced by" can" in our culture

Barack Hussein Obama the first African American President of the United States has shown us that we can do anything

My life will never be the same.

I finally understand what it feels like to be a part of history

As I pause

Allow me to relish in the moment

(Sigh)

These are the stories and experiences that we will pass on to our grandchildren one day

One day

Can you imagine how strange that will be?

And it will seem as if it were just yesterday that it happened but the truth is it won't be.

It will be ancient history and such things will be the norm because that's what life is about and that very vehicle that I speak of is change

It waits for no Man/ Woman.

Change comes and goes whether you're prepared for it or not

So stay tuned

Because the ride isn't always a smooth one

But we will get there and it will bring about better days

When our children laugh at the notion of anything less

That innocent laughter alone will bring us peace because we have carried the burdens in the generation before so that the next generation can thrive to limitless tomorrows

It is in these closing words that I feel the impact of the world and relive its sorrows

Heaven

Heaven is that special friend

Never wanting that day to end

Heaven is that warm caring hug on the coldest day

The coco in a mug

To finally be one race in a crowd of different people and not feel out of place

Heaven is seeing the most beautiful thing out of a mere inkblot

Heaven is that warm breathe on your neck after a long day

Heaven is staring at the one you love and never looking away

My heaven and your heaven must different

Because if you look through my eyes how can you envision it

It's the quiet of the moment

The comfort with the breeze

Heaven is all around us

In the birds

In the trees

Heaven is a beauty pageant without contestants

The day draws to an end and you're reminiscent of it

That's what I call Heaven

Intentions

I want to be better

I want to do well

These are the very actions that pave the road to hell

I'm sorry

I apologize

Yet I feel no remorse

I'm the darkest part of ones character

With a flame that burns brighter than a torch

The world cries

The clouds tear up

We call it rain

It may douse it slightly

But does not extinguish the flame

My desire remains intact

I would have done things so differently

If they had gone a different way

Does that mean that ultimately it would be the same?

Fate

Please explain to me what I mean?

My subconscious responds

I'm not sure what to say

I pause

It seems like we will never make progress

He interjects

We already have!

Just because it is not immediate

Doesn't mean that the necessary steps

Haven't been taken because the gratification I seek is not instantly achieved

That's what he told me

I didn't understand it right away

But eventually I began to see

That's why they call them dreams

Because we just have to believe

I've believed the same dream for over 5 years

Plenty of times I wanted to give up

Plenty of times

I have shed tears

Quitting is not an option

So much has been invested

I think of it as an uphill battle

It is obvious I'm being tested

When it's my time things will go on as planned

This is the transformation from a boy into a man

Dots

It's funny how everything changes in an instant

One minute you're just sailing along in life

The waters are calm

Then next thing you know

You're in the middle of a storm

And you spend most of your time trying to figure out how you got there

Those sunny days that you once took for granted are now long gone

And you would do anything

To just have it's rays peek thru the clouds

Let alone light up the entire day

Life has become bleak

Pessimism fills the conversation

And paranoia of self, causes the conversations to began and end differently for you

Because you're no longer the center of attention

You're nothing more than a point in the conversation

Overshadowed by the clever remarks

Made to keep the audiences attention

You're faded

Jaded and like a scorned woman full of jagged edges

But you never meant to be this way

Yet it suits you so well

As if it were tailored to your situation

Which makes you wonder

If you were meant to suffer alone

Because you have no friends

You're so lonely

And withdrawn that you don't even have enemies

Because you're completely detached

Utterly out of place

Like a disc that makes contact with a magnet

You are destined to be erased

Anger

An uncontrollable anger

An unforeseen rage

As clearly in view as articles fill a page

A day of nothingness and an accomplished sleep my toe
touches the water I'm already in too deep

The day breeze passes and the night soon settles

A mind full of stories

But not so many riddles

Do you see me?

As I see myself

Actions and equal reactions in the order as holes in a belt

Enchantment

Love is sitting on the porch

Just thinking about life

Sitting there

Holding hands with the possibilities of her being your wife

Life is full of things we don't understand

But it doesn't matter as long as you're here with me

I just need you to hold my hand

Hold it tight and never let it go

Separate we're weak

But together who knows

We can tackle the world

But let's take our time

I have everything I need

As long as you're mine

If life were a video tape

I'd press rewind

So I can look in your eyes forever

Until I go blind

Fixed Change

A fixed change

A soluble anger

Addition, subtraction

Still no remainder

Locked away secrets

I dare not tell

Like a burning fire

Yet no smoke I smell

Thoughts a mist

My first kiss

Passion struck

I never pictured this

Tell me your secret and I'll tell you mine

What would you do?

If this life we could rewind

If fate were in an envelope

Would it be in your direction?

Trained in security

But you yourself need protection

Glory

The darkest edge fills the most space

Confronted and questioned about so many things

I wish I could just erase them all

The embrace that I once longed for feels different

And I identify it with the loneliness of the times in which we live

I myself am the most negative, positive, motivated and despised person that you will ever see

With fans who hate to like me because they're not like me

Which gives them more reason to dislike what they can never be

These are the very things that help me determine the differences between us

 I long for days when talks of prosperity and success are nothing more than the side bar of the conversation

Because we're all experiencing it

Instead of being accepted

I am widely criticized for what I don't do

And what I have become in a general sense

I literally don't care

(Except when it's coming from the ones I love)

I guess even at my age I'm entitled to dream of bigger things

Most of which will never be

Because we live in a world where people lack the zeal, to be anything more than what they already are

We look up in the sky for them

But the truth is we're the stars

So how come we all don't shine?

It is only when I close my eyes that I understand the truth of society

I named my pen instead of myself because I fear the notoriety

I waited for this day to come for so long and it's finally here
and I feel like I missed it

Not to get too specific

But I feel distant

Broken

Unenthused by its allure

I can still see the inhabitants of the residence

But truthfully

My foot is out the door

I can't take it anymore

I'm bored

Rather disappointed

The potential to be more

That never became anything except the next argument

Once a social butterfly

I have regressed back to a caterpillar of the times

Not only in appearance

But movement as well

I can't tell if it's true that we failed

I'll say we just didn't pass

Maybe the grass is greener on the other side

What does that matter?

When I live here

The tears I shed will nourish the lawn

Because for so long I thought I belonged

Only to discover that everyone is out for themselves now

I'm out for me

Family will always be family

But this day will not always be the same.

I patiently waited in hopes of giving her my name

Too bad I was dreaming

Have you ever

Have you ever

Locked away a bird that wanted to fly

Laid on your back and looked at the sky

Closed your eyes and started to dream

Then when you awoke things weren't what they seemed

I understood the misunderstood and questioned the unquestionable

To be unequally yoked but remain on the intellectual

To be hurt by words and destroyed by the truth to not agree with the course of life and not know what to do

To feel the deep cuts in your skin

Like butter with a knife

To reach out for the earth and be to far away

To try and hold on to something and still not get it to stay

Have you ever

Infatuation

Love

It's so intoxicating

It just consumes you whole

You go from complete control to utter chaos in an instant

But

Would you honestly have it any other way?

My life is a movie with no end because every time I see you it begins a new

I once felt all alone

But now I have you my delicate flower

I don't want to think of you as an Angel because that would be too easy

I'd rather view you as a Swan so exquisite

As you maneuver through life

Not currently mine

But any man would love to have you for a wife

You're so enchanting

I can only hope to be that lucky

Is there another word to describe beauty?

Because I feel limited by words in describing what I see when I look at you

Is it possible to love how a person sleeps?

If so

Then add that to the list

I remember all of the talks we shared and our first kiss

I don't want it to end

So I stay focused on the beginning

If only I could stay fixed in the moment

But if that were possible then it wouldn't be life

 It would be a dream

I love you and adore you more each day, of every week

If I can't think thoughts of you

Then I no longer want to think

Annoyed of my reflexes when I my with you

Because just the sight of you causes me to blink

I'm constantly overwhelmed

You're like a drug

A high that I just can't shake

A hold I just can't break

I'm not sure if it's beautiful music

But with you it's love I want to make

Damn

I miss you

Slow Burn

Like a slow burning candle

That will eventually burn out

My emotions consume me blinding me to the outside world

In which we live

My current social status correlates itself to when I first came here

Nothing but silence and solitude

Nothing but utter confusion in which I point my finger

As if I understand it

Like I'm the one calling the shots

I sit and watch as others pursue some uncertain destiny

That they believe lies before them but the only thing I see in my near future is nothingness

For that is what makes me

Because it is what we all started from

And

Billions of cells later we're able to refer to ones state as self and that's what drives me

The dissatisfaction of life

Which propels the little cogs and gears inside to grind and make this machine called the body go

Never wanting to stop because my purpose is unfulfilled and that's the only reason I'm here

I'm not scared

I just fear that what others fear will never come

And what is expected

Has already happened

This is life

Pain and misery and all its distractions

Liquid

A liquid reality

A forgotten future

A questioned past

Strange but true, ecstasy at last

An angel without wings has walked into my life

I haven't the money but would pay any price

Amazed by her splendor

She stopped me dead center

Neither east nor west

North or south

No matter how hard I thought

No words came out of my mouth

Love is in the air

Let me take a deeper breath

It was when I met you

That everything made sense

A touch in your reality

Without fingerprints

Moonwalker

The man that once did the moonwalk

Now walks on the moon

Plays in the stars

He died too soon

We watched him transform

Over time as if he lived in a cocoon

He couldn't be stopped

He kept rising like a balloon

They say the good die young

Does that mean that the bad live forever?

He put the "S" in superstar

That's why the rest are in lower case letters

I understand grief

But I cannot feel his families' pain

To us the "King of Pop"

To his mother Michael just the same

God has a plan for all of us

I am a believer in that

He took the stars of old

So that new ones, may grace the map

Don't be too sad take time to grieve

Just don't forget his legacy

Because for every song played the world bleeds

The "N"

Nobody cares

They steer left of my pain

They run and they hide

So they don't take the blame

Mind state altered

Mind bionics physically lifting me up each and every time

I smile and joke but things really aren't fine

I cannot tell night from day

Because my eyes remain shut

To what goes on around me

I'm drowning

The raft thrown in

But I'm too heavy

Christmas melodies ignored

The holiday surreal

Not in the spirit what so ever

I figured if my head remained below the covers

Then it would be over quicker than it began

I was wrong

Can you help me?

Niggers

I remain because I'm great

I suffer in the world because they hate

I never give up because I persevere

If I seemed relaxed it's because I don't care

If you hear the whispers

Those are the voices of the non-believers

Half breeders

Chronic under achievers

They see us

But what they picture in front of their very eyes disgust them

Because we're moving on in a definite direction

That direction is up!

It's not about Obama

It's what he embodies

He's proof that we're more then gang banging, slang talking, pants sagging, gold front wearing 26-inch rim riding Niggers

He reminds White America of what they never wanted us to receive and that is an education

Because they fear us

If they could just lock us off in the woods they would because they hate to be near us

I'm a captive only in my body because my mind wonders free

Move your hands from in front of your eyes and maybe then you'll see

Don't listen to them

It's up to you to be whatever it is you want to be

Set your sights on a goal praise God and you will achieve

Pectas Excavatum

I died because I wanted to see

I lived because I wanted to read

I learned to breathe without air

I never looked back because they didn't care

I bust in the room faced with stares

It didn't matter because you weren't there

In this world I'm without cares

I just want to cuddle up like a bear

Not a transmission

But I've switched gears

Alone for the most part

I don't embrace my peers

I would cry but that requires tears

I keep speaking but they cover their ears

They rather not hear

I wish I could take off on a Lear and just jet away

If I died tomorrow

Why should I live for today

Not like you would care anyway

Because these days are different

The page has been flipped

Reminiscing of warm embraces and soothing kisses have become far and few

I looked thru the crowd and now you're brand new

At times we were one but ultimately remain two

It all happened so fast even I'm not sure what to do

The lights flashing, I guess that's my cue

To many a king but to you just another dude

She was talking while I'm reading

I'm not surprised she's rude!

Shadow talk

The Shadows remain silent

My body is numb

My heart defiant

I feel empty

I look at the mirror disturbed by the vision because it is much different then the faces around me

Lost

Not sure where I fit in

Or if I'm meant to

I just know that a father is what I have become

But a father I never had

Just a mother who attempted to wear both hats

Utterly unsuccessful

But the attempt was appreciated

A force raised me

That came deep from within

It's as if she's never left me to this day

She humbles my spirit and leads me to pray

"Mary Artis" is her name and I wear her on my sleeve no matter how many years pass she remains right here with me

Some Things

Some things are better left unsaid

I constantly talk to those who don't care

You would think I had a hole in my head

Why haven't I learned?

I'd think that I was better off dead but that's definitely not the answer

The pain overwhelms the body

It spreads like cancer,

Causing ones state to change

And

When I state my feelings or thoughts all I get is scattered applause and laughter which mimics the actions of the non-believers

Who see what they want to see

Which am certainly not I...

It is only this paper in which I share my thoughts

That allows me to be free

For it has no face or identity

It's the best part of me

These words I write

For they are impartial and they always seem to find

The right place as I transfer them from the subconscious to this scribe

If I die

I will never totally be forgotten

Because my words will keep me alive

Life is a mystery to some

A quest for most

We're all feeding off of something

Are you the parasite or the host?

Why be boastful

When you haven't accomplished much

We're all on display for his amusement

When will it ever be enough?

The day soon becomes night

The young have now become the old

The world will end

Just as it began

Will we return to the ash?

Which we once called home or will he open the gates and show us the throne

I guess we'll never know

Until it happens

Life is full of uncertainty

And intentional distractions

. Com

No heart felt apologies here

Believe me

I do solemnly care

They think I'm weird

Because I stand out

 Now I'm the one they fear

Pay attention

Things have changed

No longer just an article

My life's front page

No saves or reset button

This is a coming of age

A rage much worst than the streets

Like a mad dog

I warn you by showing my teeth

Yet they continue to move forward

I've given various excerpts of my life but it goes unnoticed

Try and understand the craft

I am a poet

This is effortless

My ability is not seen because I don't feel the need to impress the simpletons of the

World

So I tend not to show it

How deep is life's ocean?

I guess you will figure that out when you start to drown

Because you will reach out for help and there won't be anyone around

(Who needs friends)?

I am a witness to my own demise

Surrounded by fake, phony, people, like shit is with flies

An endless swarm

More annoying than anything

Because they can do me no harm

After all, these dudes play tough and act out through text and instant messages

My classroom was the street

I never viewed Myspace, Aim, BBM or Facebook as a weapon because I always had my hands

Maybe to them, it's more of a coping mechanism

Shout out to all you cyber surfing terrorist

Maybe I will wear grey for a year straight to alter your plans

I can't take you guys seriously

Because the line that you said not to cross was written in sand

The Corp.

We claim to care but when things get tough

We turn the other cheek

Words of righteousness without the equivalent action just become another good speech

We fall short every time

Not because we can't compete

But because we don't truly understand the game

This was done to us on purpose

Yet they refuse to take the blame

I care for all people no matter nationality color or creed

God has placed me here to close a void

To fill a need

I was only a child when she saw that I was different

I gave her my word that I wouldn't disappoint her

And I meant it

My struggle is fueled by purpose and directed by determination

Thru me she lives

She has been reincarnated

She is the car

I am the driver

E.V.O.L

Staring in her eyes

I see the future

No

Our future

So I thought

It turned out to be the land of make believe

I cry inside

Wishing Hoping

That maybe one day

She would see what I see

A life filled with love

Happiness

A family

I know we both longed to have

Sharing times

Where we would just stop

Look at each other

Smile and Laugh

Only wanting the chance to lie across her chest

My head snuggled between each breast

Listening to her heartbeat

Not missing a second

While she touches me so sensually

Giving me chills

That go deeper than deep

Causing a sensation overload

I had hoped

In the future to look into our child's eyes and see her face.

Thinking

Believing

Knowing

That after all this time it was worth the wait

Something is different

Something is wrong

Duh

It's called reality

And it's finally kicked in

I find myself just sitting in this car

My car!

Stuck helplessly in love

Not traffic

Still wondering what happened

Knowing that there is no "us"

There is no "we"

Her and I could only go but so far

And our expiration has been reached

I talk so much to my partners because I aim to teach

But even I wasn't aware of what truly lied beneath

She could never do any wrong in my eyes

I believed all she said

Knowing it was lies

She was my definition of purity

How pure

Obviously

Not pure enough

I longed for her touch wanting it needing it

Even though it hurt me so much

Never

Say never

Because I'm far from naive

I just put my intuition in the back, and allowed my heart to take the lead.

Now do you see why I don't dance?

They say, "It's better to have loved and lost than never to have loved at all"

Which is true

And in the face of adversity stand tall

Because at some point in time

Even Angels must fall

Did you get that?

Just think about it

After all is said and done

Titles, Situations, People, Arguments

Are irrelevant

I would've remained by her side to the end of time

Even if hell froze over and pigs were able to fly

It's what I call Unconditional E.V.O.L

The Experience

To experience true love and never know

To watch it melt away in your warm hand like snow

To forgive and never truly forget

To unlock a heart that was covered with cement

To love someone but not like them all the time

To have everything screwed up and on the surface seem fine

To give her all the chances and the world good are bad t

To be accused of being like a father but never really wanting to be her dad just a friend or maybe even a lover

To extend the same love as you would for a sister or brother

To see the end ever since the beginning and not understand

If only we were unimaginable

Like the sum of grains of sand...

Technology

What ever happened to kind greetings?

Questioning ones day

Articulate conversation

Knowing exactly what to say?

Now we hide behind technology

It has become the barrier that insulates us all from true interaction

I tried going one week without my device

It was the hardest thing I've ever done

How did I make it to this point?

Just to regress with my obvious dependence upon something once thought to be so frivolous

Which has since then become somewhat of an appendage

I remember when you would rub my face or stroke my hair

To let me know that you missed me

Now you send smiling faces and emotions to kiss me

We stand right in each other's presence

Yet we type space and send and in the process of that all we remove ourselves from each other's space literally

Never getting back to what once was because it can no longer be

We've been smothered by technology and it's convenience

We were just too blind to see.

I don't need virtual reality

I rather get back to my own sense of self and desire to interact because soon I will forget the appropriate gestures

(Idk) if I'm mad then it will be capital letters

Still typing not sending

Not sure if to delete or make it a draft

Way pass go

I stop only for a second to catch my breath and reflect on a time when were all happy just to have simply things

Now phones are labeled boring if not equipped with custom rings

I stand up against you

Not afraid to show my face

I am different from the others therefore I cannot be erased

But just in case I backed up my life plan on an external disk

So if I go missing then they will get my gist

The list goes on and on

But the pages reflect very little progress

It makes me wonder

Are we viewing the same things?

Chronologically the same ergonomically different

I can see the similarities but why should it be up to me to list it.

They say we're all gifted but at what?

I was never good at math but never came up short with my money.

Always liked the slim ones avoided the frumpy types goodnight is heard out in the distance can't place it with a face maybe it's my imagination that is playing tricks on me

How is that when I'm awake?

Original ideas

When I'm the one who's fake!

The Prequel

These nights seem longer because you're not here

The air I breathe is thinner

I can see the silhouette of your body in the distance

I'm stuck in my position, not sure if I should move closer or just enjoy the view

Your beauty consumes me with vacuum like precision

My eyes are closed but the vision is perfect because it's you

I can't believe

This feeling of love that I have been allowed to feel because I threw in the towel on happiness years ago

And

Here I stand fulfilled

Relieved

Reborn and overwhelmed

I always wanted this but now that I have it

I'm not sure if I deserve it

The lights are dim

My vision blurry

I see a face in the distance

Your face

It's like the sun married the moon, it's such a beautiful sight

Your eyes big and brown swallowing me whole

Not leaving anything behind

Your skin like silk

Freshly spun

My mind wonders like fingers through your hair

I'm totally out of my element

I've experienced many things in this life but this.

This is different

I'm not sure if I'm prepared

All I want is your happiness

On the darkest of nights

I see your smile and it lights up my life

Music is playing that I've never heard or could imagine

When I'm between your legs there is no activity between my ears

You're my only focus

My palms are sweaty not because I'm nervous, but because I'm enjoying the moment

I can't kiss your body enough

I don't want to miss a spot

Let my saliva be your moisturizer

I smell something and it's not smoke

Its freshly released sex in the air

I want to take a deeper breath

You're close to me but not close enough because I want to breathe your air

Exhale what you exhale

Feel what you feel

The fire burns with no wood the day comes with no warning

We're intertwined like a game of twister

No energy for a rematch

Let's call it a draw for now

My soldier covered with cream after you leave my lap

Too bad I'm out of chips

I can't get enough

Your breath on my cheek sends chills all over

It's like your body was custom made for my hands to explore.

Look at that ass

With more cheeks than the "Lost Boyz"

Your body has more curves than a racetrack

I want to take another lap around

I'm not comfortable with a draw

I thought about it

I'm ready for another round

At the very moment the bell rings

This whole time it was just a dream

If that's the case

Where did these panties come from?

If only I could remember her name

I have to get home so I can go back to sleep

The Proclamation

A blank sheet of paper full of words not sure what they mean

 They fill the page as brush strokes fill a canvas

They connect seamlessly

In just the right places as if they belonged there all along

Just as you did when I first held you in my arms

Now you question my position

As did those before us question Jesus...

I do not proclaim to be on the same level

I'm simply making a comparison of the endless cycle

I label as thought

If I were an antenna I'd have the best reception

If a provider

Then I would cover all the land

If a way to heal then I'd be the cure

I would be the hand that starts the stopwatch

Because not all good things come to an end

They just take on a different path

It is up to the user to identify with it

And if they cannot then it was never really the right fit for them after all

You look at the surface and it misleads the mental

Because we find ourselves perplexed by the mask worn by us all

Figments of ones imagination

Not truly understanding the inner workings of the spirit

Which intern does not even began to explain the psychological movement of the mind and it's precision

If a clock then it would be of Swiss movement

I am true to these words

As the clouds are to the sky

I write down parts of me for the world to witness

The evolution of a man and to leave some understanding to the child that is yet to come

When I return to the sky

The body dies and the mind becomes numb

Believe

To believe that you know the truth

And not even be close

To not have no real resources

But learn to make the most of what you have

Is my family my own are did you take my place

To look at yourself in the mirror and not even recognize your
own face

Can someone pinch me and awake me from my grief

To be so tired and not allow yourself to sleep

Why count sheep when you can ponder of endless days

To see the most amazing site before you and not even be
amazed

Does life hate me or am I destined to be great

All the convictions and certainness in a man

Who never had faith?

Believe not what you hear

But what you feel

In the end the darkness is the truth and light surreal

Can you enter my temple without permission?

I think not

How is it on the coldest day?

You still seem to be hot

I'm bothered by my own thoughts and am subject to
interpretations

Confused in a world of ideals and immoral infatuations

Vision

You can't see me but you can feel my breath

In the dark I am the company that allows you to sleep

During the day light hours I am what keeps you alert and motivated

Throughout the day

You tell others that I exist but they don't believe you

Because my face is not present

I am the voice in the ear of the skeptics

I am of the shadows the now, the past, the memories of those that once were

Now

It's just us her and I

She can't remember what it was ever like to be alone

Because I've always been there omnipresent

It's almost like we're the same but through action and experience it's evident that in fact we're different which is expected

As long as a mean is reached

But this may be out of reach for the short arms of society and notoriety is forgotten and replaced with neglect

Supported by doubt of what will never be

Yet I find the slightest hint of hope

Which drives me to continue

But if you truly don't like the program

Simply change the channel

Divided

We are divided

By more than just seas

Why don't butterflies mingle with bees?

Don't believe everything you see

Believe this world is driven by greed

How come the poor stay poor and the rich get richer

I don't like what I see but can't alter the picture

If only I could tune out

Maybe even change the channel and move on

But I can't forever trapped in the poverty of my environment

I cash out on the riches of the mind

In due time

I rewind and decline

The declinations of past hope because I'm a loser another
thinker added to the corner trapped in a box with no borders

Differences

What is change?

Is it the same as different?

Or is different the same as change

Can we call it other?

Or should it have the same name?

Some call it magical

Some call it love

Others call it a mystery

I really just want a hug

Causation

It's a real issue

Eating at the fabric of your very being

Seamlessly eroding your life away

Like cracked pavement that lines the streets

The salt that is spread only causes further damage

We attempt to patch it up

But it will fall apart again

The next time worse than before...

The inhabitants riddled with a foul odor

That consumes the air

Causing one to gasp for the next breathe

Smothering our neighborhoods with flags and violence

We lay victim to your constant menacing

Because we remain silent

Silent...

To the point where it becomes unnoticed

But it can easily be seen if you look close enough

The degradation of our own

As white America watches patiently

As we self-destruct and then point the finger

It has lingered amongst us for over a thousand years

Countless events and endless tears

I was told that I was the future

So I guess it stops here

Some of use this environment as motivation

Food for thought

That feeds the hunger to free them

So they may escape and attain more

You just have to believe

 As she did with me

At a very young age and even now I continue to progress even though she's not here to see...

A Blown Candle

What is love?

Is it the same as pain?

Are the processed in different areas or localized in the brain?

I've done my fair share

I've contributed to many broken hearts

But you always feel it the most when the one you love ends up tearing yours a part

You can't brush your shoulders off enough

You can't erase the pain

I just want permanent plugs in my ears

So I never have to hear her name again

Once thought to be my best friend

Potentially a wife

She was the one I loved most in this world

And still she stabbed me in the back

Simultaneously piercing my heart

I was one of the greatest teachers

Guess I wasn't really that smart after all

I saw all the signs and disregarded my visions

I should've listened to my gut

I know what they truly mean when they speak about intentions

I plan to move on with my life

I intend to do well

I'm never looking back in her direction

She can go to hell

I get the message that I was once to young to read

Women love with their eyes

What's in front of them?

Men love with what's below their waist

I gave 5 years of my life to a stranger

If only I were an Ostrich

I would bury my face

I refuse to turn my back on love

I was fooled by what appeared to be a beautiful butterfly

Turns out it was nothing more than a well camouflaged slug

So full of disdain

She'll be hard to get out of mind

It's okay because everything gets better with time

The candle blows out and the room grows dark

It's not that I'm dead but mentally

I just need to restart

Bliss

I'm the me in we

Which together makes us

I give what I can

But for you it's not enough

This time seems rushed

I'd rather it stand still to collect my thoughts

So you can understand how I feel

Everything said was real like the numbers on a bill

Did you feel that chill?

Shit

My Coolata

Just spilled

I loved what you loved

Liked what you liked

Then why do we fight?

Sleep in separate beds at night

You are where you are and I remain just the same

My feelings are tangled

You confuse it with a game

I've never liked spiders

Always hated webs

It's all in my head

Do you get what I said?

I'm not J. Holiday

But I'd put you to bed

The first thing remembered is usually the last thing said

If that's the case then follow my lead

I traveled through life and watched my heart bleed

Was given the knowledge

But never wanted to read

Motivated by greed

It ate me alive

Anything is possible with you by my side

Anything is possible as long as you remain

Whether it be as girlfriend

Friend or wife it's a title just the same

Life is too short don't waste it playing games

Caught up on a title that can easily be changed

It is the feelings that play the major part

Instead of worrying about a title

Wonder if you have his heart

Burdens

Light as a feather

Yet the burden I carry holds so much weight

It bares down on my soul

I carry it with me every where I go in hopes of unloading it

Making it someone else's problem and no longer my own

But still no offers

I feel guilt for my actions and thoughts

Why is it in order for me to feel joy I must inflict pain and misery upon another who could be my own sister or brother

Mother definitely not a father because that would lead me farther into the dark preventing my escape from my burden

I'm uncertain of what tomorrow holds if it holds anything at all for me

I'd rather not think about it

I'll just experience it

That's the only way I will truly be on my way

These days I experience more of the same

Meeting different faces but they all have the same names

I'd rather not try to explain

The situation to you with words

Because it would only confuse you

Giving rise to thoughts of confusion in your mind

I sometimes sit and question God even though this is not permitted in hopes that he will give me insight into things that are beyond my reach

To teach me to soar above the clouds swim in the deepest waters easily these things I do not wish to do physically but mentally

To embrace all and reject none

I wish to encompass the thoughts of the world and fulfill it like the sun

The Cast

As I cast upon the shadows and forget where I stood

Living in posh surroundings but still reminiscent of the hood

Amazed by what I was yet too see

Right in my face but still couldn't believe what I was destined
to see

People all shades and colors united as one reminded of Martin

But turned off by the sound of that smoking gun

Chaos

My passion is effortless

My desire is unconscious

I brainstorm with no thought,

Yet my mind manages emotions

Feelings and thoughts

With a side of anger

I'm different but the same

I'm sarcasms nemesis

I feel pain but haven't effectively learned how to process it

My tears are dry

My eyes heavy

Nobody likes me

Yet they all claim to love me

Sometimes I just want to be alone

I can't feel my face

My heart weighs heavy

My expression is blank

The lights flicker in the house but nobody's home

My personal life is non-existent

Why doesn't anything good every happen to me?

How come it worked for him and her but not me?

Do you understand what you're reading?

I'm my biggest mistake

I cause the only problems that I have

Because I don't know when to say when

I'm surrounded by cronies

I don't have any friends

If I were writing instead of typing at this point

I'd be switching pens

Will it ever end or am I destined to continue?

I'm faced with the same problems

Even though I opted for a change of venue

My puzzle lacks all the pieces

These thoughts are not my own

I wanted to pick up and call you

But couldn't dial your number on the phone

Why is it you don't see?

I find myself jumping to more conclusions

I tried to cut out the pain but the knife was dull

I don't want to hurt anymore

I can't take the pain

I really just need a hug

I fell flat on my ass in life

Cats don't always land on their feet

I pulled it out kept in my hand

But couldn't bring myself to beat

I guess I really am off

What a dick

Constant Variables

Finally it's over

The agonizing pain that renders me senseless has ceased

I wonder if I'm dreaming or am I truly free

Everything seems different to me now

Even this place called home, it's no longer a home to me

My body is present but my mind wonders free

Searching for life's mysteries

The pendulum still swings but in no certain direction

Yet the momentum is constant

If this is a sign of things to come

Then I'm no longer optimistic

I've noticed that when you least expect things

Fate strikes and something or someone is placed in your path

Each drawn in sand because they can be easily washed away

Nothing in this life is promised

Not even tomorrow that's why I live for today

Consumed

Consumed by the rage from within

That drives the monster that I see before me

I wonder

Can I continue on this seamless path of pain and frustration?

As this black hole called my life that manages to suck in even more unsuspecting victims

I hate this life

I wish that I could just press pause and right my wrongs

But if I could it wouldn't be life, at least not mine

I rewind and sometimes cue my life but the tape always seems to catch up because the pain from within is destined to come out

Pain and misery is what my life is all about

Our Darkest Moments

Our darkest moments

Are full of things

We don't know about and don't understand

When nothing seems to work and we definitely don't have a plan

No course of action

Totally unsure what to do

All alone in the world and it's nothing we can do...

You extend your hand for help

But nobody reaches back

To be surrounded by people called friends and none have your back

Our darkest moments are those that are not seen blinded by stress and motivated by need

Just

Wanting to lift your head above the water

Because you don't yet know how to swim

To be in a class of others and not know where to begin

Ever lay awake and think of all the food in the world and not have anything to eat that's what I get for playing by the rules

Next time I know to cheat

To savor the taste of steak

The saliva dripping from your tongue

Caught up on these false thoughts

The only thing you're chewing is gum

If we could get full off thoughts

Then I'd like seconds please

To have nothing to eat and be accused of cutting the cheese

I keep waiting for my turn

But the only thing I get is skipped

The smile on the surface does nothing more than masks the truth

To be so unhappy, lost and alone and not know what to do

These are our darkest moments

You pray to God for answers and direction but he's not returning your calls

To be right near the edge of life and not want to fall

They say he never gives more then you can bare

Then why is all this weight on me?

Even though he doesn't answer my prayers strangely enough I still believe

These are our darkest moments...

When friends are far and few

But voice mails and answering machines are easily attainable

Because now that you're down

You're all by yourself

But you can vividly remember those days when you were so quick to help

How could you forget?

That's the story of your life

But now you're down

Seeking pay back

They wouldn't think twice

Life is one big circle

Then you're pushed out

Once your numbers called you're forgotten about

These are our darkest moments

Darkest 2

It seems like Virginia was so long ago

But

Now these days seem closer together

I swore I'd never fall that low again

But it seems that I couldn't totally keep my word

The account might be different more zeros and a strange value in front but emotionally I feel the same

People are strange creatures

They thrive on dependency and I myself rather be independent of these connections

I cannot even break free of these webs entangling me in the bullshit and frustrations of life

The higher you get the harder they want you to fall

But what if your skyscraper view originated from the ground then what?

I hit the ground running and seldom looked back

But still acknowledged the past and the alliances that were necessary to forfeit defeat

I'm still here more determined than ever the names the same just added a suffix Sr.

But

The process is Elementary

I see the faults in individuals before I even embrace them and I still consider them good company

Because I've learned to embrace the shadows to envision light you must understand the dark

Back to people they turn their backs

Ever so quickly

The forecast changes

Good thing I bought my umbrella and my goulashes because this shit is going to get deep

My journey is far from over

A certain piece of paper hasn't found me as yet

But I'm certain it will

Because it just feels like this is my moment

 Where I can just say fuck everyone

I did it!

With God by my side

The haters are allotted front row seats

Because this show is invite only and I only want those who pretended the most to attend

Fake friends who had their own plans for my failure and a dependent crisis that was narrowly avoided

And now I avoid them

More toxic than second hand smoke

I choose to hold my breath

Because the air they breathe is ugly

Alone that's the way I came

That's the way I go

I don't long for the end because it's definitely coming the when and how one never knows

So I keep on my toes

These words are true like the sharpest knife and here we go the curtain pulls back watch the show

They never expected me to host

My very appearance leaves the audience is froze

Guilt

Tranquility speaks to me softly in the right ear

While the left surveys the crowd

I find myself...

Overwhelmed with shouts of we're the lost souls

That it's too late

Ringing in my ears

Filling the inner cavity with doubt.

The cowl covers his face

But his eyes expose his soul

There is no understanding or comprehension for his actions or appearance

Just know that he's all business

And that his business is our shortcomings

We strive for more

But we never seem to get it

Which causes us to develop a defeated attitude

About what's meant for us

And the only experience that we experience is that of never experiencing happiness...

It's not that happiness is not meant for us

Because happiness has no preference

It's just that some of us do more to obtain it

While others wait for it to drop in their laps

Keep waiting because it will never be

We seldom get what we should at the right times

And this causes us to fall short of what is expected

Leading to more self-pity

I pity those whose daily task consists of more excuses

When will we acknowledge our own problems?

And began to make a change

My guess be never

I've seen so little change in 26 years

I no longer cry tears

I just stare until my vision becomes blurry

In hopes that when I blink what I see will be different

Space

My life is the same as it was and has never really changed

I view life as a book as I flip another page

Embraced by few

Discriminated against by many

I have few people to call friend and it leaves me feeling empty

I'm not sure why I'm disliked

Unsure why my company is not wanted

Maybe I'm cursed by good looks

This life can be daunting

I just want two real friends to call my own and a home with at least two cars

Life is my spaceship

Goodbye

I'm off to mars

Chatter

A time capsule that I couldn't swallow

A thought I couldn't shake

A feel

A touch reminiscent of her warm embrace

She is the past now but I once thought she'd be my life

A long-term girlfriend

That never amounted to a wife

Climbing a hill of beans will get you nowhere

I chose the elevator this time and skipped the stairs

But the stares continued

As the on lookers pierced into my very existence with things that I couldn't understand rumors and chatter it was hard to make clear

I stared hard at the window but couldn't see thru the tears

Everyone knows me

Yet my age likes and dislikes are a mystery

I pass them in the streets

Yet everybody misses me

A bull's eye with no target

A plane with no runway

Just keeps running

I will figure it out one day

But until then you think of something

A Sycophantic Ideology

What I feel on a daily basis is different

I have moments of anger

Others are full of happiness

Life's' jubilation

Others dark constrained and chemically erased

My position is stereoscopic on life's balance beam

I manage to teeter thru this tunnel of fixations

That I neither understand nor want to

Because I'm not fixed on any

I want what I want and have what I don't necessarily need

What I write is meant to enlighten

To comfort and challenge the reader

If every third line is read and the others forgotten

You will simultaneously see what I really am and that is challenging at best

I'm nothing more than an instrument that has been instructed to relay messages

That is instructions for life

What life is up to you?

The vehicle has no wheels a motor gears and is full of fuel

Do you understand how it moves?

The screws are loose the frame badly bruised it's eyes shifty but still allowed to move

Oxygen depleted

Nitrogen abundant

Remnants of a carcass are illustrated through signatures

But the outcome is inconclusive

The shoes are tied with loose laces

His hands rinsed in dirty water

His eyes full of pain

Yet his tears are pure

I am Miseries Company on the loneliest of nights and loves
partner when hate is busy

Read this with closed eyes and see what I see

Then die because you won't be missed

If the shoe fits then

Why not wear it?

When it rains the world cries

Because it starts with a single tear then multiplies

Life's caterpillar

In a world of butterflies

How ugly is that?

Hollow Thoughts

Wind blowing in no certain direction

The breeze still

Chills run up my shoulder

Blank stares from all those around

Profound laughter within

Not shared with the spectators

Misguided rage in a bottle

We call it hot sauce

Edge of your seat action with no preview or ticket to buy

Best seats in the house

For a show that will never play

Heartburn and indigestion off of these thoughts

The complication of love and heartache

We all search for the same happiness

A crew with no compass

A journey with no certain conclusion

Malignant dreams in a benign world

Which shutters change with negative connotations as   "
Nigger" or "Slave"

Our ingenuity they fear

Our talents copied

Our achievements stolen

Erased never to be seen again

Trial and many errors brings a conclusion

But to what

I rather not dangle my feet in the pond

I'll stand firmly on the ground in my own space

Similar to a cul-de-sac

You're all invited to take refuge here I have plenty of seats

All the hair the same color

But each strand different like snow flakes

I embrace all of these ideas that I've managed to capture on this scribe

I want you to see what I see because in your own shoes you're not alive

You're in that in between place when the soul dies...

Imagine

Imagine your life without a face

A lost soul trapped in this place with no identity

No beginning no end.

To have your life is like a dead end street and others tell you there is a way out

If so, then why are they still here?

Because the truth is there is a way but it's not meant for us

Our purpose is not to be happy

But to suffer at the expense of others because if we came up what would become of the working class

No longer subject to his burden

We could say kiss our ass and finally unmask and acknowledge the true sentiment and spirit found in our culture and abandon this tumultuous nature of the nigger

But if that ever happened

What would we be called then?

If we as a people were no longer associated with the title of the nigger?

What would we be called then huh?

We would be called free...

Incomplete Expression

Have you ever fallen in love while sitting

Not able to find the right words

But have written a page

Overwhelmed by another's presence and made to feel like
that of a younger more juvenile age

I have and it's because of you

I just wanted to know your name

Everything else

Was more so a dream

I have these fantasies where I can just have anything

But all I want is you

I find myself peeking in to the minds eye with thoughts of
grandeur

Wondering through a field of roses with so many different
flowers

Yet I pick you

I began running in no certain direction constantly looking over
my shoulder

But still not able to shake this feeling of joy

Your lips like warm silk freshly spun

Your skin an oasis and my lips seek water

Intensity

My cup Runneth over

I miss you

Please come salute my soldier

He's friendly but bites like a cobra

I'm horny

I want to touch you all over

Exploring your body in the smallest crevices

I called you

Did you get my messages?

I dreamt about

Maybe cumming in your face

Draping you in pearl necklaces

I'm full of recklessness

I have no boundaries

I'm on a journey in search of good competition

Just listen

Come challenge me.

I follow the twist and turns, moving through your valley

It's slippery

I'm looking for buried treasure

Your walls are astounding

So arousing I can't get enough

Whoa

You keep it on display

Not in a rush the sign reads

Look but don't touch

You gave me an inch

When I really wanted a mile, it doesn't matter to me

As long as you smile

I love you

Love

Love is timeless

Love is unstoppable

Love is grand

Like piano keys of the heart

Love is something we always dream about and are lucky to experience no matter how difficult it may be because it strengthens the heart

Love is like quicksand; once you're in the midst of it you're trapped

Utterly stuck

Love is like a symphony in your heart with no instruments

Love is standing still, simply savoring the moment

Love is that feeling that you feel when you're feeling it and you

Can't stop but you want to because it hurts sometimes?

But for that reason you can't stop

Let's you know that it's real

Love is you and I

Love is God

Love is life and life is love

Because it is seamless extraordinary

Special

Eventful, hurtful and annoying

More importantly it's unexpected

That's what makes it great

Love is like water

It has no definite appearance or shape

Love is like fruit on a tree

Take your pick

Love is like that icy road

If you're not careful you'll slip and even though it may hurt

What is love without pain?

Now wipe yourself off and get up and do it all over again

Love is the words to this page

That has been achieved without a pen

Love is that warm hug on the coldest day

Whether it's between loved ones family or friends...

To me love is 1924 and 1114

These are the numbers that mean the most to me

Invisible Scars

Postponed dreams and wishes...

Accelerated misery and pain

Disdain on the faces of all who enter this small space

Their voices bounce of the walls

Causing a residual or an echo to some

But to me it is clear as can be...

I read the book from the end and wonder about the beginning

Because to me life is looked at the wrong way or too many ways

Which leaves us at a standstill

Still I try to free the minds of the masses with their carpet grass roots

Because they have no idea of the system that plagues this land or the others

We're all interconnected

But it is just that which keeps us apart

Like magnets of opposite polarities the closer we get it becomes more apparent that it will never be

If it did this world would cease to exist

We're trapped in a game that we can't win

Forever enemies

Lined with hope on the quilts of doubt

I make my mark

I was always taught it's better to turn on a light than to curse the dark

(Man will destroy himself) and the suffering we experience
gives the soul meaning and allows one to truly appreciate
better days if they ever come

Ruble

It's funny because so long ago this day meant something

Now it's nothing more than the day those two towers fell

A day that tore not only a city but also a world apart

Grief stricken family members try to hold their heads high for the ones they lost but at any cost they remain fixed in time

Settled in the rubble that still remains in their hearts for the fallen victims and heroes of the day we call 9/11

Angels in heaven

They are now

They circle the crowd and each drop a feather from their wings

To replace the hurt and the scars

To let the people who love them

Young and old

Know that they have not forgotten them and we call them clouds for that is what masks the sky

Because they have traveled afar and reside with the most high

In his hidden but obvious palace in the sky

Jargon

Darkest sentiment realized

Past thoughts forgotten

Relieved of my misery over come with pain

Fixed in this space called home ostracized by the masses

Over looked by family

Misunderstood by my partner

Criticized by friends embraced by strangers...

Revolutions per minute give me the strength to move forward, seeking, wondering not yet understanding

The steps necessary to reach the end...

Eyes full of bitterness

This vessel called a body over extended abused utterly tired of the perpetual cycle of life

End of the line thoughts trapped in a perfect circle

Goals failed frustration imminent, danger around ever corner

Empathizing with those similar to myself

Yet different tie dyed thoughts limbic movement casual conversation with ones self

Identity crisis shrugged shoulders at my pain constant turning of the cheek

The pain consolidated

Compressed by anger evaluated daily

Aggression misrepresented in ones action

Intellectual stability lost.

I lack sleep grief stricken because of the prior mood

Fuel on empty

PS3 or 360?

Day or night

Left or right

Bitter or sweet

Straight or crooked

Even if I spoke it in plain language you still wouldn't get the message

2:59AM

It's 2:59 am few seconds from 3 am

I find myself staring at your number

Written on a crumbled up piece paper

Buried deep in my pocket...

I wonder if you're sleeping, maybe you're wide-awake

Making love to him but whispering my name

Seeing my face and feeling my body

These late night fantasies are taking over

Possibly even replacing thoughts of my present love

Damn

Only five minutes have passed but I find myself staring at the clock

Slowly time creeps by

My heart beats fast and my breathing gets heavy

It's now 3:07 am

I can't take this anymore

...........I'm calling you

Right before I dial the last number

My Blackberry rings

It's you

Sounding sexy

Soft voice

Filled with the same enthusiasm as myself

3:10 am

I'm wondering do you miss me

You wish I were there?

We continue making small talk

Both trying to get to the point

Avoiding our purpose

Making it even more interesting

3:15 am

I'm undressing you

Slowly

Whispering sweet nothings

Hearing your soft moans

Makes it well worth the wait

Knowing I can please you better than he can

Not in a rush

Giving you descriptions

Of soft touches

Silk sheets and burning candles

Tell me your desires...

You want me to kiss what?

Lick where?

Sure baby it's about you

Your fantasies

Your demands...

I can hear your background change

Your breathing changes

I can hear noises

You got music playing

Anyway back to the moment

I'm not touching you, but is this cheating?

By 3:25 am I wish you were here

We have to do this!

Lately you said it's been hard to get away

By the moaning on the other end

I can tell you're playing with passion

Don't stop until you explode

My soldier is at full attention

Waiting for your commands

Marching back and forth

3:50 am

Did you cum?

How do you feel?

Can we have more than this?

Can I touch you with my hands and not just my words?

These fantasies are they possible?

4:00 am

Confession

I want you in my arms, not in my dreams

Laying in my bed...

Wearing what you came into the world with

I want to explore your body

Giving you kisses from head to toe

Not missing a spot

Come on be selfish

I want it to be all about you

Your feelings

Your pleasure

Closed eyes

Music playing that probably caused our existence

Not in a rush

Nothing extra

Just me... You

Your passion and my soldier

4:21am

A knock at the door

Disrupts my thoughts

It's you

Last Call

Life is unfair

I mean that and I don't care if this rhymes

You meet so many people in life

 Some just not at the right times

They stare in your eyes so innocent full of love and full of glee

You stare at what they're staring at but you don't necessarily see what they see

What they see is stripped down perfection without a flaw

No matter what you did in life to them you will always be pure.

They just crave your presence a kiss or a hug, yet you shy away

I was taught to be brave bad and bold

I was raised a different kind of way

I never learned to embrace my feelings and exchange kind words

As old as I am I pause

These memories have left me disturbed

It's true chronological order is expressed in the sequence of events

I was taught to throw stones

I never learned to pitch a tent

The pieces of the puzzle are given

But not always in order consider it the luck of the draw like having a son or daughter...

These feelings I foster are dear to me like a child

I've grown tired of the life once lived

No longer do I wish to run wild

My life was like a subway

Many people have jumped this turnstile

I have so many memories

If measured by length they'd go on for miles

I just saw the most precious thing the other day that no word could describe

You ever have so much to say that you're limited by words

Because what you're feeling and thinking they just can't express

Just thinking about it causes me to hyperventilate

Now I'm out of breath

It is these rare stumbling blocks in life when you have to improvise which truly make you feel alive

I doubt you get what I'm trying to say

Because most never seem to understand

It was an accident done on purpose

Because its purpose has already been determined and it is when the darkness comes to light in life that I will finally close the curtains

Lemonade

My fingertips numb

My heart remains warm

I haven't seen the forecast

But I've weathered the storm

I've been told lies

But ultimately

Sought the truth

I held the tightest grip

But still couldn't free the screws

I've been alone before

Many times I've been betrayed

I've stirred my thoughts before and drank them like lemonade

I no longer care

I view life different

Some say it's a walk in the park

Then I'm due for a visit

Now I live life by the hour

I no longer count the minutes

I write down my thoughts if not I'd for get them all

I am the best to ever write my pen is my sword

Do you want to die?

I have been reborn

Something came over me

Something I've never felt

I gave up on my friends and asked God for help

His words have set me free
I'm no longer afraid
It's getting hot out here
Want some lemonade?

Posture

I asked for food

They fed me hope

I asked to be cleansed

They gave me soap

I wanted a sense of meaning

They handed me a dictionary

I didn't understand my purpose in life

They helped me create a Monster account

Everything all seemed to come and go so quickly

They removed the clocks from my room

I said I wanted to rise above my problems

They gave me helium and a bunch of balloons

I wanted to stand out in life

So they made me a neon sign

I asked what was next to come

They told me to be patient that it will come in time

I asked for love they showed me the first season of Ray J

I told them I wanted to leave

They gave me a compass

I needed direction

I told them they gave me a map

I complained that I didn't feel respected

He asked me to look around

I was the only one that was naked

Completely stripped down in life

Because instead of trying to do it by myself

I became a victim of the system with a hand out constantly asking for help

Get over yourselves people

Lost Expression

Let me be your leisure

Your relaxation

Let me be your pillow

My words your blanket

My arms your sheets and my chest your mattress

Close your eyes

You can be my passenger

I just want to drive

In no certain direction, just enjoying the ride

Full of gladness

Smiles from ear to ear

I keep on my seat belt for safety

Not because I'm scared

At life's rest stop

No need to refuel or check the fluids

I've been down this road before

When I find what I'm looking for I'll know what do with it

The crowd goes silent and the man tips his hat and exits the stage

To see the truth in plain site and not even be amazed

Life's amnesty

Without negotiation

To you just words

To me nerve impulses and lost sensations

An abyss of nothingness

And constant manipulation

135

SEX

It's different yet the same for each of us

Something more than just a rush

The whisper in her ear that makes her warm to the touch

Slowly

Stroking my finger tips up and down the crease of her back

She doesn't have to say a word

By the way she curves I know she likes that...

She slowly takes my finger and rubs it gently across her lips

Then places it in her warm mouth sucking on it

Just enough to get my attention

It's as if someone plugged me into a socket because I'm
definitely turned on

But she won't let me come any closer

She blindfolds me with her head tie securing my hands to the
bedpost

Putting her in complete control

Maneuvering over my awaiting body

I quiver at the thought of her letting me go

She gyrates her wet pussy just an inch or so over my mouth
with the sweetest nectar

Dripping on the bottom of my lip...

I'm not in a rush

I patiently wait for more to come down before I steal a taste

My soldier is ready for his orders

Standing at full attention

She welcomes him with the softest kiss

Just below the tip, she knows me oh so well

Each kiss causes my soldier to swell that much more

She asks if I like it, but before I can respond she placed her fat juicy pussy on my awaiting face...

It fit so snuggly in my mouth as if it was meant to be there

And just before I could savor the moment

She put my hard penis in her mouth

The intensity just got turned up a notch

Since her pussy was occupied with my face, I placed my lonely finger in her asshole

It grabbed it with vacuum like force

Her pussy is getting even wetter

As I nibble on her clit

Just when I think it couldn't get any better

She cums right on my face

I have the got milk mustache without the flatulence

I break free from my restraints and slam her on her back

Spreading her shaking legs and massaging her warm clit

With my super hard penis teasing her

I place the tip inside

I can feel her walls contracting trying to lure me deeper into her pleasure center but I resist making it even more stimulating for the both of us

Then when she least expects it and is just about to give up

I jam my manhood deep into her awaiting hot steaming pussy

Her mouth opens with a scream as if she just won a million dollars

But she's been rewarded in another way

I'm pushing her body to its limit with each stroke

She grasps her belly

I slow up wondering if she's had enough but she tells that I better not stop and assures me she's up to the challenge

I slowly work my free hand around her neck gently choking her as I push my plug further into her socket.

I turn her over on her belly

I can see glimpses of her perfectly shaped ass from the minuscule light provided by the moon that peaks through the window

I can feel myself about to explode just before I do I snatch my slimy cock from her dripping pussy and I ejaculate all over her belly spelling my name

Pestilence

The "Shadows" are amongst us

But I'm still breathing

The crowd is growing

They're still seeping

My words are going

They're still feeding

You don't get it?

Probably because you're not reading

I just want to survive

But they keep on

Keeping on

I will not stop

I just believe that it's much bigger than I am

So keep reading

There will always be injustice in the world

It keeps us even

Pay attention to the words I'm writing

Try to be descent

We are his servants

 Ask for forgiveness

Surrounded by so many

But when it comes time

You will be

Your only witness

Mirror

I stare out the window in lives daze

So many words coming at me I can't jot them all down

So much noise and chaos I don't recognize the sound

The rain covers the window I look out

The world cries

A new life born somewhere joy happiness is felt, somewhere else another dies.

My feelings fill me up like water

Yet I can't get a hold on them

The randomness of my thoughts separates my reality

I sometimes feel alone but this feeling shouldn't be new to me

Because I like the rest we're born this way

It was nothing more than the Lords' preparation for these off days...

The disappointments of life no longer disappoint me the same

I take responsibility for my own actions

No longer making excuses

I listen on a different tone and see things in my own perspective

I'm dejected

Erased

Lost

Found and embraced

Empty content with nothing and filled with his word

My heart weighs heavier than normal

It has never been easy for me or anyone else but I refuse to let that stop me

I've done the unthinkable

They still don't believe

It is when and only when I look in the mirror that I see and understand the simplicity of life and how good it feels to be free

Mirror (Extended)

I stare out the window in lives daze

So many words coming at me I can't jot them all down

So much noise and chaos I don't recognize the sound

The rain covers the window I look out

The world cries

A new life born somewhere joy and happiness is felt

Somewhere else another dies

My emotions fill me up like a pitcher of water

Yet I can't get a hold on them

The randomness of my thoughts separates me from reality

I sometimes feel alone

But this feeling shouldn't be new because I myself was born this way

Just like the rest of them

I view it as nothing more than the Lords preparation for the days to come

The disappointments of life no longer disappoint me the same

I take responsibility for my own actions no longer making excuses

I listen on a different tone and see things in my own perspective

I'm dejected

Erased lost and found

Embraced

Empty content with nothing and filled with His word

My heart weighs heavier than normal

It has never been easy for me or anyone else in my family

But I refuse to let that stop me

I've done the unthinkable

They still can't believe it

It is when and only when I look in the mirror that I see and understand the simplicity of life and how good it feels to be free

Freedom comes at its own price

Some are not willing to pay the high cost

The random glances have since become long obsessive stares

Until it is my own image that I loath

My attitude has taken a turn for the worse

My aptitude is low

I'm not sure if I can tolerate the choices I've made

Why is this mirror judging me for my decisions and mistakes?

IT'S JUST A STUPID MIRROR!

It's not the boss of me

It doesn't make any choices

It just carries the reflection of what it sees

I stare in it so long eventually I see nothing

Because that's what I have become

Literally wasting away

Life and time passing me by because I spent it all

JUST

LOOKING IN THE MIRROR!!

Mistake

Deafened by the screams

Constantly ignored

Mistreated abused laughed at

Isolated by the pain

Circumstances not always known

Just happy to be here

Not certain where we originated

Tired of the questions

Confronted by lies consumed by misery

If I was made out of love then why is the blanket that covers me lined with hate and anger

Never knowing the whole truth

Just accepting that things are different and never will be the same as other families

No hugs here

Just foul words and constant swings to the abdominal section

Eyes covered with whale fat to conceal the disgust of our presence

Yet all we wanted to be was loved and appreciated

Constant looks in the mirror trying to figure out what we did

So much going on in our young lives never getting a chance to be a kid

Oasis

Past discussions trigger new intentions

Mind abroad domestic visions parallel ideals

Faulty answers

Ambiguous questions inappropriate methods

The nature of the hostility increased, sensation lost while the pain persist

Invisible boundaries restrict me from reaching my true potential

Hidden truth about my past mask my future

Caustic measures extend my solitude and causes my spirit to surrender

The devil finds delight in my frustration

God urges me forward limited understanding leaves my mind somewhere in between

Stomach rumbling

Butterflies cover the scenery

I gasp for air as if the supply has run short

Palpitations, moist brow palms sweaty vision disturbed words jumbled Consciousness fading

I linger on because if I stop what example will I have left for others

Little sense of direction

All I know is that I serve a purpose agonizing in light of my own epiphany

Not sure of what I've become

Experience leaves me bland

No further recollection of the moments past

Just long blank stares in to the world of someone damned

Who was but will never be again

My Dream

I prosper because I believe

I have insight with closed eyes that allows me to see beyond the trees

I may not always get what I want but I have what I need

To be trapped in life's library and not be allowed to read

My heart is empty but still bleeds

When I die

The head stone will read helped other of all shades colors and ethnicity

An angel without wings

And that

Today the world has truly lost a kind soul and then the phone rings

But I don't answer

The words are like cancer eating at the hearts of those, whom cheated me.

Attempting to Parle my dreams

In long term parking

I sit in determination lane with my hazards flashing because I'm not leaving and I will not stop

This freight train of success is on a one-way path and that is to the top

So either by a ticket or get out of it's way

The conductor only has 4 senses

Sight, touch, taste and smell

I dare you to make a sound

What is convoluted in our hearts will never leave you see it

when you sleep
They're called dreams
What's yours?

Testimony

The Lords Words

Intimidate some but they motivate me

We're divided by nothing more than ourselves

Fundamentally we're all the same

Yet we're all different

Our diversity is the true embodiment of His vision

But we poison it with thoughts of hate and prejudice

Which ultimately sets us apart

Just because we're all created equally doesn't mean that we must all look the same

We are all made in His image and blessed in His name

Amen

Only takes 4

We're surrounded by words with many different meanings

But do we L.O.V.E

I doubt it

Its only four letters but (full) have so much meaning

Yet we abuse it

(Love) is four letters the same as (work) which you have to do at love?

To make it

(Last) which also contains the same number of letters

But many of us (take) also four letters this for granted

Which leaves us right (back)

Which has four letters where we started and so much (time)

Also four letters is (lost)

Another word with this amount of letters

Don't think that the whole concept of love is too difficult

To understand

(Just) realize we never give at the right times

It's supposed to be (ours)

Yet it ends up yours and (mine) and we (find)

Which has four letters that it wasn't love in the first place

Because with love comes understanding, patience forgiveness and compassion (over)

Which is four letters (time)

So if you took time also four letters to read my thoughts on L.O.V.E.

(Then) don't which also has four letters

Let it (pass)

Which is four letters because you (will) which is four

Letters (miss), which is four letters (when)

Which is four letters

It's (gone)

Orientation

Things are so quiet in my head

My outward expression gives the appearance that I'm bothered by something

Obviously I'm not

I keep walking on

This shadow that follows me is not my own

The steps behind me grow heavier

I'm so full of disdain

I can't bother to take another bite of my sandwich

It's 830pm but unfortunately I'm still out to lunch

I sit and stare

At memorize of old

My stomach growls

I should probably eat something

Am I the only person that thinks it's warm in here?

Does the ice warm the drink or does the drink cool the ice

Hey

This room looks different

Did you move the furniture around?

My circle has corners

My visual field is altered

Have I fallen out of perspective?

I tried to make a paper airplane but it wouldn't float.

I walked sheep and counted dogs last night

I really want a hot cat with relish on a potato bread bun

I think I have (BPH) because I keep getting pissed on in life yet, when it's my turn my stream isn't strong enough

I only eat Kosher

Are you out of napkins?

I think I'm full

Why is Santa using mules to pull his sled?

Is it really that cold in Denver?

I fill totally out of place in this situation.

That's what I get for fraternizing with beginners

Proliferation

I've been called strange

This is probably because I don't understand myself

I didn't have anyone to talk to

A silent cry for help

The cards dealt have frayed edges

I'm not out the window in life anymore

I've abandoned the ledges

Unlike Heath

I guess the "Jokes" on me

Those around me constantly laughing

I was too blind to see, what they see

My posture is different

You don't need a big red nose and funny shoes to be considered a clown

Never exposed to water

Yet I feel I've already drowned

They tried to throw me a donut in life to save me

But I wasn't hungry so I didn't eat it

They told me I wasn't who I thought I was and I couldn't believe it

If you didn't get my message

Maybe you should go back and reread it

On life's space bar

Bound to be deleted

I don't want empathy anymore

You can keep it

I wish my shadow would have a change of thought

Because I don't want anyone to agree with

I'm so lost in my own puzzle of thoughts

Company is not needed

My life is one big abbreviation

Because I've run out of words

My work promotes discrimination

Because I only write it for the mentally disturbed

If you feel we don't have this in common

You could just be a nerd

Think about it

My ideals are translucent yours non- existent and the relevance of the situation is no longer relevant to you because you're so immersed in nonsense that you seldom know whether you're going or coming

I sit and watch because I'd rather not make a spectacle of us both

I prefer to watch

The minds perversion of sorts that encompasses the entirety of my ideas

I slipped on many bananas in life

 None of which were peeled

The dynamics of the process of colliding action potentials between my ears conjures thoughts of things cataclysmic and that's not what scares me

What truly scares me is that I'm the only one that has escaped the box and views things in an alternate perspective

Which I refer to as reality

Pushing Up Daisies

Will you take this man to be your blank?

I don't really want type the rest, just hinting at what I think

Did I mention that I'm stressed?

My tanks on empty and I'm broke

Yet I'm full of life

What was I thinking typing that nonsense?

Who would want to be my wife?

A life of duh

Hmm and I can't remember her name

They don't tend to take me seriously

They think I'm playing a game

That's not so

The rules are gone and here I just remain

I sit in the dark and speak of the shadows because it helps me hide my pain

The Economy is not the only thing broken

So is my Heart

I wish life were like a video game and I could just press restart

I've given so much

Seen so little and made many mistakes

Yeah I'm a little better off now and for that

To the Lord I give thanks

I'm the greatest and the worst

Most captivating jerk that you ever will meet

I'm the reason they invented seat belts because my presence keeps them on the edge of their seats

I'm so suspenseful

Too bad you can't tell but I've loved you for a long time even before we knew each other's names, I had visions of you being mine

Dancing in eternity

The music so serene

I empathize with your situation and I hope that it will change this is not your life, it is just a phase

The disdain fills the air

I think I will hold my breath.

I've given everything to this life

I've lived now

I think there's nothing left

I can hear the wheezing when I breathe

My lungs are full of noise that's not the laughter of the crowd

They're standing with applause

The show is over now too bad we parted ways

I've looked at the calendar recently and it's full of better days

Salvation

My mental efficiency is equal to that of a Prius

My thoughts parallel to your reality

I read the books from the end to the beginning

It's more interesting that way

I experience time differently than the rest

I don't see hours and minutes

Just months and years

I'm not sad but I cry tears

I am listening but don't want to hear because the world is ending faster than you think but you're too simple to know what to fear

You ever look inside a stove and watched the flame

Well

That's what in store for most

If the rules are not followed

My heart blackened my soul hollowed

I go on my own because the path of others is too dark to follow

I live for today because I've lost faith in tomorrow

Scenery

My mind is lost in thoughts that are yet to be created

Infatuated with ideas I am yet to think

Distracted by a vision that I have never seen

Puzzled by a question that wasn't asked

Enlightened by a suggestion that wasn't made

And disturbed by the outcry that was never vocalized

Forgotten by those who never saw me

Loved by few and loathed by them all

I sit and watch

So that way I will never fall to my enemies

Sitting

I was just sitting

Waiting

Looking off into nothingness and then I saw a star but it shined differently than the rest

It a had a certain twinkle that caught my attention

So I kept looking and as I did it appeared as if the star was looking back at me

Because it seemed much closer than before

Yet I wasn't afraid so I kept looking

Eventually I stopped because my eyes became tired from this back and forth staring.

So I looked away and when I looked back it was gone

At least that's what I thought because it's been years since I've seen something that held my attention so strongly

Well not until I met you

The funny thing is you're just like that star such a beautiful sight miles away

I cuddle my calendar counting the days until I can touch you like that star that once seemed out of reach

You possess a calm that not only relaxes my body but also settles my mind

Time with you is nothing more than hours minutes and seconds because your presence causes it to remain still and I'm filled with this feeling of feelings that has me feeling strange about you

I've never experienced a look in your face or a caress of your skin.

This is insane these thought that I think of a long distance love that in reality is only a short distance away

I'm sitting at this intersection of life lost in thought and

You come along, don't know much about you

But something about picking you up doesn't seem wrong

A touch is nothing more than sensory perception

But with you it feels different

It feels much stronger like it was always there and it always will be...

So therefore I've closed my eyes and allowed myself to see

I'm dreaming this dream

Time and time again

Waiting to see

If it will ever be

Truth

Guided by truth

Restricted by laws

I've dropped jaws with metaphors and opened closed doors

With my tabernacle type approach with out ever taking a seat

My heart beats a loud and my words are not discreet

Do you get my purpose?

If not then why question my message

This hood sermon leads and drives others of different colors

Uniformly sisters and brothers and stirs the melting pot of the world

Until it falls over

Now we lean on shoulders with the impact like boulders

Because this is heavy

This is the beginning of the end the walls and stereotypes have been broken

I am considered an artist

Not just a token Negro

Sycamore

Skin broken thoughts intact, the minds pendulum in constant propulsion

I don't necessarily understand what any of that means

But I do know that I have to continue because agreements have been made and I have more than 1 promise to keep

The Sycamore tree bares fruit but nobody eats it

I don't worry about the spectators

I just intend to give them what is not expected

My minds eye sees nothing but happiness for me at the beginning, middle and end of the day

The time I spend here is not my own

I borrow it from those who are yet to come

But truly believe in me

The clouds form pictures that are not readily identifiable to the naked eye

But I see things way out of perspective

My refractory period lacks the necessary mechanisms of adjustment so I interpret things at my own discretion

These fixtures that remain aren't fixed on anything nothing more than a prelude to an unforeseen end that will surely come

My tank is on empty but I'm full of hope

I just hope that it's not wasted because people lack the zeal to acknowledge anything that's not readily available

And that I am not

Conference Call

I had a conversation with self

My conscience told my shadow not to look at me in that tone of voice

I didn't speak one single solitary word but my voice was hoarse

Life is full of so many options and still I couldn't make a choice

I had the best navigation that money could buy and I'm lost

I saw an image of Santa Claus but the pole he was near, wasn't north

Even though we all seem alike we're cut from different cloth

Some as soft as dryer sheets

No need to mention their names

Unnecessary attention given to the weak tends to ruin the game

In this life you don't have to be tough, just surround yourself with lames

And when things don't work out you will know who to blame

I dreamt of a beautiful face but couldn't remember her name

The texture of her skin was soft her voice angelic

But I was cheated by time because now I'm awake

Life is dynamic

It seldom gives you what you want

Just because your hand is in the cookie jar doesn't necessarily make you caught

Lighten up!

The Game

I hate when I cry

My tears fall to the sky and the clouds touch the ground

And when frustrated

I yell and it doesn't make a sound

My words are profound and when I whisper I'm always heard

People get distracted

By the surface

And how I mastered being a nerd

We read the same books but are on different pages

We see the same things but are moving at different paces

I'm on cruise while you mash on the pedal

I'm more R&B, you're Hip/hop Rock and Metal

The clock is broken so the hands can't be turned back

You are not alone because I too feel whack

This was supposed to be love

This was supposed to be bliss

I realized exactly what you were when I got past your kiss

You're conniving

Sneaky

A liar just the same

You think you're ahead of the curve but the truth is I invented the "Game"

Whisper

A whisper is but a soft sweet sound

The sound of your voice fills my heart with undying passion

A glimpse in your eyes sends a mans mind into a fantasy

In which he wishes were so real

Your touch sends chills through places one never knew existed

You feel like the softest smoothest silk

That I would never let go

Your lips are like the soothing wind on the hottest day

Cooling my face as the temperature rises

Your body is like an hourglass

All you have is time

You're like the most delicate flower

With such sweet nectar

That is gathered and passed from bee to bee

Even though all relationships aren't what they seem

I still close my eyes and allow myself to dream

Whisper (Reloaded)

A whisper is but a soft sweet sound

But the sound of your voice fills my heart with undying passion

A glimpse in your eyes sends my mind into a fantasy

That I wish were real

Words don't come easy

My pen slowly travels across this paper

Not sure what the next line will be

So much time dedicated

In hopes of creating a work of art

Locked in my room

Windows closed

And the only sound is silence

I question God

Asking him for the right words to describe your beauty

Your lips are soft

With a kiss that's soothing

Like the wind on a hot summer day

Your sexy shape reminds me of an hourglass

Enjoying your presence as time creeps by

My delicate flower

Blessed with the sweetest nectar

You remind me of a sunset

Beautiful

I look forward to seeing you come and hate when you leave

You possess a rare personality

There's something about you

That inspires me

You open my mind to new thoughts and ideas

You're young women

With an old soul

It's as though you lived this life before

Passing your knowledge onto my listening ear

Anticipation brings me to you again

The next day

Eager to hear your thoughts

To hear the story behind every tear drop

And to experience every emotion

Your words bring me closer and take our souls in unison to a far off place

I sit quietly in disbelief

Questioning my own reality

Knowing that all relationships aren't what they seem

To have love like yours

It would have to be a dream

The Set

They think something is wrong with me

I find myself sitting

Staring

The screen broken

But the TV still plays

It's not what the screen holds because my minds trapped in a maze

I flip the pages in no certain direction yet you still understand the story

I am a condemned soul these poems are my legacy

The words the worlds glory

Please don't read this and make it a negative thing

I'm so happy when I write

My thoughts these words mean everything to me without them I don't know if I'd be all right

The placement is perfect the conjecture is felt

I am like margarine under the heating lamp of life

It is certain that I will melt

When I say melt I don't mean in a literal sense

I mean I will cease to exist and the only records of me being here will have to be retrieved from prints

I'm finally close to getting up and no longer staring at the set

I've come to terms with many things

No longer full of regret

After you left things were different at least so they seemed.

I now refer to you as dictionary because you helped me

understand what they mean

I loved you more and more as the days went by

It was inevitable that I'd lose you like everything else

Why did you have to die?

I guess you were better off with him

In your home in the sky

See when you die it's not that peaceful because you see all the pain of the world while you lay still

Ever stare into their eyes that glazed look fills your body with chills

It's okay following me

I will lead you out

I'm sorry

I lost my way because the plug to the set just came out

Tivo

My therapist tells me I need to lighten up

So now I try to laugh at his jokes, but even that's not enough

When I go to the market the milk purchased is only 1 percent and this month on purpose I was short on my rent

Then after all this he states that's not what he meant

He proceeds to call me a blockhead and said it was hard like cement

I think cement is solid

Fixed in one place

I'd rather be described as water because my thoughts require lots of space

He told me my head was in the clouds. I told him because I like to take planes

He asked me several questions I only asked him one and that was what is your name?

It made me feel uncomfortable to talk about myself

I read one of those books

But it was no help to self

I feel even more lost now

Than I did before I opened its pages

Now instead of just having suicidal thoughts

I gargle with razors

Life is like old fruit just stick with it until you find the part of it that's good

People claim I think I'm better because I no longer live in the hood

I'm frustrated

Delighted

Indifferent just the same

I should've taken my Ginkoba because I still can't remember his name

My brain is scrambled and my thoughts are fried

I was just reading the paper

Yeah

Another white person died

Freeze the Jews

Burn the Germans and put the Blacks in control

White people are like couch potatoes

They refuse to let go of the control

They want to shut us down

Stop the Obama campaign

They use articles for campfires anything bearing his name

Mc Cain is hell revisited

The demon spawn

It's a waste to elect a fossil for president unpreserved it won't last long

We've finally trimmed the Bushes now we can envision new horizons

Can you hear me now?

If not

Your service should've been Verizon

The now network won't save you later

Anything positive you do will always attract haters

I say shoo fly shoo get the hell out of here

What do we as a people care about?

Rain

We've all ready shed enough tears?

The Epiphany

These days seem closer together the happy times have gone away

I watched the forecast but there are no signs of them ever returning

That and I once thought that the burdens were lifted I was free

I've come to learn that it's not true the problems have simply been compiled on the side reserved for me... (Future agony)

I care to a certain extent because I know it's out of my hands agreements dissolved my life voided like a hand that was unshook

The deal is off ringing in my ears confined to the darkness of life

My back pocket where I hide my tears

God has a plan for all of us

Wow (sarcasm)

I must be his favorite because the hardships that I've faced for the past 25 almost 26 years has filled the pages in the book of life, way past the margin nights in the cold homeless mentally and physically starving...

I decided to beg his pardon then backed off it because with him there's no use arguing

The jargon that I'm compelled to spew separates me from the reality that pains me as the words are being entered the soul bares some relief but I can't keep going on like this...

When will it be my turn or have I already been skipped

It's fucked up when you're constantly told how much potential you have then end up not doing shit

The Broken Umbrella

My words are seeds

Let them grow

I've plowed the fields of the mind without a hoe

Things are different

You didn't know?

I've managed to gain momentum in life like an avalanche

I promised to keep going and never look back

This is my chance

I move with such certainty

It leads one to believe I've lived this life before

I've had many doors close on me in life and never once did I become discouraged

I just learned to climb thru windows

The venue has changed but it's the same menu

My mental is focused on things that don't yet exist

Like a Thunder Cats Movie

Call it Preemptive foreshadowing

I want to go, like Dorothy clicking her heels

My unwillingness to embrace the others around me has caused the tension to rise

It manifests in such a way that I'm starting to think it's more than just this situation

It could possibly be stemming from something else

An Internal paradox in cabinets that are locked open

Leaves one under exposed

In the background a great symphony plays the song with such

joy and compassion but they have no instruments

The sounds produced are stimulating to ones ear.

Yet

I can only read lips

Bummer!

Why is that when I cry my tears flow backwards?

Why do people use black umbrellas to block the sun?

I always thought dark colors attracted the most heat.

And in knowing this we wonder why the cops are always after us

Maybe it's more than "Racial Profiling"

Could it be Physics?

I doubt it; we're just their personal quota fillers in life

Either that or we're just special.

So special that

They setup random checkpoints just to give us a ticket!

Instead of a ticket why not give us our reparations

Imagine that?

Thoughts

Troubling thoughts

Loose concepts

Misguided truth past interpretations

Yet I arrive at the same place

I foreshadow my life editing the previews and deleting some scenes

That lay parallel to ones finale...

The mission altered

The reception superb

But I still feel empty

For this is a mere step in the process of completion

Which will define me and allow my character to evolve into something

That the world has never seen

True passion and desire in its purest form

The thunder lightening and cracking of the sky before the storm

TSOL EPOH

I'm so tired

But

I don't want to sleep

I take a deep one but don't want to breathe.

I don't like words

Is there another way to read?

I'm without money

Maybe that's why I'm not motivated by greed

I'm psychologically congested

Often tested

My mind trapped in thought

Mentally arrested

By some detested

She admitted it

Confessed it

I can't be bested

They don't understand my methods

Psycho power exist

Even if you don't care

I speak of being a farmer seeds I sow

I'm not scared

You want to read outside the lines

While I read in between

I type constant thoughts

But you don't understand what they truly mean

Thought like ice cream full of flatulence

I expel these foul intentions because these are life's accidents

I attempt to reproduce feelings

Some out of anger

This could of all been prevented with some antiseptic and a sterilized hanger

Do you disagree?

Then why not beg my pardon?

What I'm giving you is food for thought

In a world that is mentally dormant

Transition

Life's wreckage

Fuselage everywhere

Time spent picking up the pieces

Inadequate conversation

With ones' self

Mentality distilled

I'm capsized

Compacted

Just like a pill

These chills run deeper

Much different than before

My life is wide open

No longer knocking at deaths door

I've found my way back

I admit I had help

The pattern altered

Rearranged in my head

Only able to pronounce vowels

I no longer want to understand

My passion has evaporated

Never to be seen again

I hope to die on the toilet

Then this shit will finally end

Homeroom

The lights dim

My vision blurry

I see a face in the distance

Your face

It's like the sun married the moon

It's such a beautiful sight

Your eyes big and brown swallowing me whole

Not leaving anything behind

Your skin like silk

Freshly spun

My mind wonders like fingers through your hair

I'm totally out of my element

I've experienced many things in this life but this

This

Is different I'm not sure if I'm prepared

All I want is your happiness

On the darkest nights

I see your smile and it lights up my life

Music is playing that I've never heard or could imagine

When I'm between your legs there is no activity between my
ears

You're my only focus

My palms sweaty

Not because I'm nervous

But because I'm enjoying the moment

I can't kiss your body enough

I don't want to miss a spot

Let my saliva be your moisturizer

I smell something and it's not smoke

It is freshly released sex in the air

I want to take a deeper breath

You're close to me but not close enough

Because

I want to breathe your air

Exhale what you exhale

Feel what you feel

The fire burns with no wood

The day comes with no warning

We're intertwined like a game of twister

No energy for a rematch

Let's call it a draw for now

My soldier covered with cream after you leave my lap

Too bad I'm out of chips

I can't get enough

Your breath on my cheek sends chills all over

It's like your body was custom made for my hands to explore

Look at that ass

With more cheeks than the "Lost Boyz"

Your body has more curves than a racetrack

I want to take another lap around

I thought about it

I'm not comfortable with a draw

I'm ready for another round

At the very moment the bell rings

This whole time it was just a dream

If that's the case

Where did these panties come from?

If only I could remember her name

I have to get home so I can go back to sleep

Polarity

It's funny how everything changes in an instant

One minute you're just sailing along in life

The waters are calm

Then next thing you know

You're in the middle of a storm

And you spend most of your time trying to figure out how you got there...

Those sunny days

That you once took for granted are now long gone

And you would do anything to just have its rays peek thru the clouds

Let alone light up the entire day

Life has become bleak

Pessimism fills the conversation

Paranoia of your own identity causes the conversations to began and end differently

Because you're no longer the center of attention

You're nothing more than a point in the conversation

Overshadowed by the clever remarks made to keep the audiences attention

You're faded

Jaded and like a scorned woman full of jagged edges

But you were never meant to be this way

Yet it suits you so well

As if it were tailored to your situation

Which makes you wonder if you were meant to suffer

All along because you have no friends
You're so lonely and withdrawn
That you don't even have enemies
Because you're completely detached
Utterly out of place
Like a disc that makes contact with a magnet
Destined to be erased

Obscurity

The sign reads one way

But the traffic flows both ways

These are the last days

Senseless tragedies no longer make the front page

Just articles

That read equal treatment for Lesbians and Gays

I pause

To wipe my tears

As the words fill the page

They should be ashamed

But who am I to say

I'm just a Black man with an opinion

I myself still trapped in a cage

Not really free

Just allowed to roam

We think we're their equals

Because now we're allowed to buy homes

It's the simplicity of this message that complicates things

When you read these words

A bell in your head should ring

You should strive for better things

Why sit on the side of the throne

When your place is with kings

I'm not a prophet

Just a student of the game

Even when I'm gone they will remember my name like red
paint

On white carpet

I have left my stain

Open Heart

Open up your heart and not just your mouth

Most of us are unaware of the words that come out

Complacent in your own position

Our division is subject to the shortcomings of a few

But reflects on us as a whole

I'm tired of just being

Existing in the shadows

I wish to stand apart from the stereotypes

But to do that I need others to hold me up

Because to stand out in a crowd

The others must fall

Maybe this is my own selfishness that will destroy me

I always seem to want things that are furthest from my reach

To teach is to do more than etch a sketch of knowledge in the mind

It is to trigger a reaction that fuels change

To ignite the thought that will affect the world

And it's people

And re-position us in our only position which primary

Not secondary and surely not third

To live in a world and be viewed as a minority

Is absurd

When everything we have contributed is major

I favor none but my own

I didn't ask to come here

Sometimes

I just want go home

But where is that?

I guess I'll find it when I die...

To waste youth is a crime

That you receive no sentence

But within you is the prison

That's not worth living

And for that your soul will diminish

Pro Choice

Pro choice

What does that really mean

Just a fancy term that means choose option A or B

Doesn't really mean much to you or me

But take a closer look

It's treachery

They think I don't know what they're up to

As if we don't understand

That they're not concerned about our well-being

It's all part of their plan

A scam

Fallacies of good deeds

I laugh at the mistakes made

Stirred and poured refreshing

Like lemonade

The suctioning of life from a sacred place

Uncontrollable guilt

A mask covers his / her face

The lies told to conceal ones fate

You said you were off to the movies

Truth is you had another date

The clinic is where you're headed

To destroy another life

We're not all responsible

This is a part of life

Some of us have been many times

With different people

We hang or heads low

Not able to look the one you wronged in the face

Guilt projected

Not really sure who's fault it is

To her just a kid

To him the beginning of a legacy

The next tomorrow an extension of one's self

This cloud that looms over me

I'm not sure how to shake it

I just know that it's following me

I believe that one-day

I will truly be happy

So much time wasted

Trying to love a person that doesn't love you back

A proverbial smack in the face

Heart full of disdain

The pain has now carried over to the surface

I drag myself to the mirror

To see my own face and question if I deserve this...

Fiction

Marathon thoughts

Paraplegic movement

Momentum

The certainness of the situation unresolved

The pendulum still swings

The ice around me has now melted

I'm free

I can't contain the rage

The page has been turned

The steel mill empty

Caricatures drawn

Your own conclusions

Is just that?

Your own conclusions

My postulates have been disproved or improved

These things are not relevant to an impoverished mind that falls victim to the constant bellows of contradictions in the crowd

Unnecessary References

Cindy told me she was hungry

So of course

I went to get her something to eat

A chicken burrito from Taco bell

Guess what

I shot a big ass Bear

Cindy did movies

I guess moves aren't as easy to do as they look

I just get naked

That's what I do

Her perfume has caused a ripple effect in my day

Not because I've never smelled it before

But because I'm surprised, she's wearing anything at all

This from a person that would be over dressed with a feather in her hair

I've lived to see a new year

But I'm still not sure

If I personally have been renewed

If I base it on my under garments then that leaves work to be done

Because these are the same boxers I had on last year

I wish they would stop playing that flute in my ear

Did you manage to copy down his plate number?

I guess not because if you did

I wouldn't have to ask

Untitled (Extended)

As fall draws near

I anticipate your warmth

On dark chilly nights

With only the gleam of distant stars

I envision us

My head resting on your chest

Controlling my breathing

So our hearts may beat the same rhythm

If only for a moment

I'm so in love with you

Silent yet connected

Love grows in your eyes

I never want you to blink again

I don't want to miss a second

As fall draws near

I anticipate you

The calmness of the day triggers distant memories of our first
embrace

Vigorous yet soothing

Spontaneous yet expected

I wish we could turn back the hands of time

But my clock's digital

I'm riddled with regret

That night we became one

It plays over and over in my memories

But

At this point that's all it seems that it will ever be

Is a memory?

Because you're still in love with the Sun and I await the Moon

I guess it was good to reminisce

But not dwell because it will alter my mood

Goodbye little bird

Please fly away

In my heart love for you I hold and I pray we meet again someday

I wish it were today or maybe even tomorrow

But I know it's not going to happen

I applied for a loan

Because time I wished to borrow

It's okay

I accept it

We all make mistakes

I will always be there for you

If you need me

A hero with no cape

W.I.P

The world can be so cold and cruel

I should've bought a scarf

I have so many things to say

I'm not sure where to start

It seems like only yesterday

But in actuality it has been many years

I was just learning how to ride a bike

Now I'm not even a kid

Internationally known

Domestically despised

I'm still in youthful years

But I feel I've become wise

Time changes many things

But I've managed to remain the same

I speak to the same people

They call me the same names

I don't change figuratively

But in a literal sense change is inevitable

I'm convinced that I'm different than minutes past

And will continue to evolve at no certain pace or direction

Self-inflection is what keeps the lines from becoming blurred

I love life

But don't necessarily always want to live it

Sometimes I afford myself a break

Too bad there isn't a pause button for that

I nap in the clouds and my mind wanders the stars

People judge you by such material things

Whether that is the clothes you wear or your car you drive

If only I could teleport

Than there would be no need to drive

I hate public transportation

To depend on that I'd rather die

Worthlessness

Priceless

Worthless

Two words that don't go together

Yet I feel both simultaneously

Is that even possible?

I've spent my entire life running and caring for others

But who has ever really cared for me?

Maybe they always have and it was I that didn't care for myself?

Will I ever know?

I've never been given anything in this life.

Not even Love

I had to work for that too

Whether it pertained to family or personal relationships.

I've always strived for my own

I feel empty and alone

To have a particular residence and feel like a stranger

No true place to call home

A King dethroned

No land to roam

These are all unfamiliar places and faces.

His status unknown

One day they will see the truth

In his character and it will be too late

I'm destined to rise from the ashes

Just check my birthday

It's fate

I've been here before but never this low

Constantly I've picked myself up and dusted off my shoulders

But now the scars are starting to show

I feel like crumbled up paper

Unraveled without reason

I attempted to divorce myself

I'm tired of feeling like I've been cheated

I feel suffocated

Trapped in a bubble of sorrow

Barely breathing

I don't live the same

Look the same

Love the same or feel the same

No stress is still stress so tell me who's the blame?

Is it I?

I'm still not happy with what I see before me

I feel ashamed

Is it my environment?

Is it my own complacency or is it just my own struggle with things that are routine?

I may never know

For some not knowing is blissful

But for me it may come to be destructive

My departure from all things relative is apparent

It's becoming harder to get back to happier days

When I've experienced so few in this life

Seems to ring my ears with thoughts of serendipity

But who knows

Maybe I'm wrong

Maybe everything is the opposite of what it seem

Maybe I'm really so happy that I forced myself to have this ugly and utterly disturbing dream

Lines

The lines from within

Fuel the words that come out

Powered by God

How could you ever question

What comes out of my mouth?

Determined to be great

In this land of strangers

I find myself walking on this narrow path

Full of danger

To fulfill what's been determined before I was conceived

To accomplish something great

When no one else believed.

Like rain in unison the words hit this page

Like a bull seeing red welcoming the rage

Has all the water dried up?

Or is it just thoughts of the world

When it makes it ok to dispose of a little boy or girl

Is Iraq the plaque of the world that we can't brush away?

I'm not really sure but I know someone died today...

Was he Korean, Black or White?

Does it really matter?

Because you won't remember him tomorrow

Or the day after

I doubt you will because I can't remember his name

Only time we lift our finger is to point the blame

These are not the Lord's intentions

We have been led astray

So in the name of the Father, Son and Holy Spirit let us pray!

www.ingramcontent.com/pod-product-compliance
Lightning Source LLC
Chambersburg PA
CBHW080700110426

42739CB00034B/3350